THE GRADUATE'S GUIDE TO FINANCIAL PLANNING

Ron Penksa

Rule of 72 Publishing 2020

The Graduate's Guide to Financial Planning/ Ron PenksaISBN

Contents

INTRODUCTION: RON PENKSA

The Graduate's Guide to Financial Planning (2020)

I want to start this book by thanking you for picking up this guide; an invaluable tool that can help you take control of your financial future.

Let's begin with a declaration to help you comprehend the magnitude of how important your understanding of money is to your future and why you need to start saving right now.

There Has Never Been A Generation In America That Has Had To Save And Accumulate Money The Way You Need To!

The reason I am stating this is that if you think about it, everything that your parents and grandparents have believed and relied on as a source for their income in retirement—Social Security, defined benefit plans, government and private pensions—won't be there for you because they will all have gone broke! As I write this in April of 2020, the coronavirus pandemic is causing everyone to shelter in place and the U.S. government is telling us that things are going to be okay and has sent out stimulus checks.

But the truth is, that this "stimulus" will help accelerate the failure of the previously mentioned retirement safety nets because very few people are paying anything into these sources to keep them going.

You and I can discuss or debate why this happened or we can just get on with the more important question: How do I take care of myself and my family financially, now and in the future?

In this book are some financial principles to help you understand why it is important for you to get started right now!

First, I want you to understand that saving is habit just like spending. You need to shift your thinking as a consumer to get more excited about how much you save and are saving as opposed to what you just bought. This is going to take a supreme effort on your part and unfortunately many of you will not want to heed this gem of financial wisdom. However, it will make all the difference between whether you have a sound financial future or if you become reliant on the government, your family, or charities to help you.

The idea I want you to embrace is this: Get in the habit of saving (and this is all it is, really) and to pay yourself first. Meaning that you need to start saving for your retirement right now and not a few years from now and here is why—the dollars that you save today are the ones that will compound the most for you in the future.

This book is designed to give you a basic understanding of the world of choices that you will have to make in the years ahead as you earn money and accumulate wealth. After working your way through the book, it would be a great idea to speak with a financial advisor. Two heads are better than one, and though you'll have a greater understanding about personal finance after reading this book, a professional advisor is someone who can help take your knowledge (and your money) to the next level. To put it another way, it's great to know about human anatomy, but you wouldn't try to operate on yourself if you needed surgery, would you? Of course not—you'd have a professional (surgeon) help you out. The same goes with personal finance.

The ideas expressed in this book are based on my own understanding of investment and being a financial advisor for almost thirty years.

There are no guarantees that you will become wealthy by reading this book—but think of this as a conversation with one of your favorite uncles who just wants to impart to you some of his life experiences with money, savings, and investing.

This book is based, in part, on a presentation I had given to several thousand clients (and prospective clients) over the years, designed to help give people a basic understanding of where their money needs to be positioned in order to have the most impact and why.

Isn't it interesting that one of the richest countries in the world doesn't teach financial literacy to its people? One of my mentors in the financial services industry, Nick Murry once said, "My parents talked more about sex than they talked about money, and they never talked about sex."

This statement resonated with me because in my own home growing up money and investing, or sex for that matter, was never discussed.

That said, over the next few chapters, let me, your Uncle Ron, have a big but manageable conversation with you about how you can take steps to have a successful financial future.

Let's get started…

PART I
THE BASICS OF PERSONAL FINANCE

CHAPTER 1
THE RULE OF 72

The first thing I want to share with you is called "The Rule of 72." I never learned this in school—maybe I was out sick that day—but I learned it early on in my career as a financial advisor (after I had passed my securities licenses, of course). The Rule of 72 is a powerful principle to understand and I learned it from another financial advisor who was speaking at a luncheon I attended.

The Rule of 72 is the math principle of how long it takes for your money to double. You divide any number into 72 and that will tell you how many years it will take to double your money.

So, let's say your investment portfolio is earning 9%. We divide 9 into 72 and that tells us it will take 8 years to double your money. If you have a portfolio that is earning 3%, it will take you 24 years to double your money. If you earn 12% it will only take you 6 years to double.

The same is true about interest rates on debt. So if you have a credit card charging you, say 21%, it will take only 3.5 years for that amount to double.

**Pro-tip on credit cards: Be careful when you are graduating from school. Yes, you need to establish credit for yourself and create a credit payment history, but also realize that this is not free money. When banks start sending you pre-approved credit cards, always keep in mind that you should exercise caution. You need to establish credit but not to the point where you have a bunch of credit cards and are tempted to buy stuff with these new cards that you don't really need. This is a trap that can potentially destroy you; it can (and often does) take a long time to recover.

You must pay back both the interest and the principle on credit cards. Paying the minimum will not help you get out of debt and it can be very expensive as well. Simply paying the minimums on your credit cards can become a recipe for disaster, financially speaking, that is.

Lastly, when you close out a credit card, it can create a negative impact on your credit score (wild, I know). So, when you start applying for credit please be careful as to how you use it and make sure you are in a position to pay it off at the end of the month.

I'll sum up credit cards and the Rule of 72 with a phrase I've already introduced, yet is so important, I have to share it again: The dollars that you save today are the ones that will compound the most for you later in your life. This leads us right to Chapter 2 and "The 8th Wonder of the World."

THE RULE OF 72

Take any number and divide any number into 72 and that will tell you how long it will take you to double your money.

$$72 \div 9\% = 8 \text{ yrs}$$
$$72 \div 12\% = 6 \text{ yrs}$$
$$72 \div 4\% = 18 \text{ yrs}$$

CHAPTER 2
COMPOUND INTEREST

The next principle I want to introduce you to is one that Albert Einstein called, "The 8th Wonder of the World." Do you know what that is? If one of the smartest people that ever lived called it The 8th Wonder of the World, do you think you want to learn about it?

Sure, you do!

It's called Compound Interest.

Here is how it works. Let's say you have $10,000 saved up or someone passes away and gives you $10,000. Let's just say you are twenty-one years old and when you receive this amount, you put it into a vault and don't touch it. It's invested in an account that is going to earn 9% a year. Let's do a little calculating and see what this will become after 47 years growing at 9%.

Before we do the calculation let's just take a guess. Will it be more or less than $100,000?

The beauty of compound interest is that everything doubles. So, here we go.

Age	Amount
21	$10,000
29	$20,000
37	$40,000
45	$80,000
53	$160,000
60	$360,000
68	$720,000

See how exciting it is to save money and invest it so that it grows? Don't get me wrong, I like nice things too, but do yourself a favor and create a habit of saving. Some call it delayed gratification and that is in essence what it becomes—saying "no" to things now so that you have more for yourself later on.

That is all that it is. Just like spending. It is a habit. If you only take away one important fact from this book it's this: "saving is a habit," and the sooner you start to get into the habit of becoming a saver, the better off you will be.

Let me share with you a story to help drive home the point. In the early 1990s I visited a prospective client in her home at a time when I was working for a major financial and investment institution in California. This prospective client had a portfolio where she had her home paid off and had accumulated over $400,000 in saving.

The amazing part is not that she had accumulated the $400,000; it's that she told me that when she and her husband were young, both Navy officers who participated in WWII, they each made $147 a month!

How do you accumulate $400,000 when you are making $147 a month?

Over the years they were able to make bigger salaries but the most important part of this is they got into the habit of saving at an early age.

Early on in their marriage when they first started saving they use to use envelopes, cookie jars, and coffee cans (and eventually utilized savings accounts) every month and just didn't stop. They didn't spend on impulse purchases. They always made sure to think long and hard about whether they needed something vs. just wanting it.

One other thing I encounter around saving: most people think that, "when I get my raise or promotion I will start saving." That sounds great but it generally doesn't happen. So think of it like a financial muscle that you need to build over time—start saving early and be aware when you're spending your money and what you're spending it on.

If all of this seems overly daunting, it could be a good reason to have a no-pressure, introductory conversation with a financial advisor. Someone who can possibly provide a little outside perspective.

The most important principle for you to remember is: The dollars that you save today, are the ones that compound the most for you in the future.

Today it is much easier to save with tools like payroll deduction, automatic drafts, low initial investments, and monthly deposits. With these kinds of tools it is much easier for you to get started and won't be difficult to do if you start right away. Part of the reason you want to start with saving part of your first paycheck is because if you don't see it (what you're saving), you won't miss it.

CHAPTER 3
PAY YOURSELF FIRST

Another rule that you must follow is that you must pay yourself first! Let me say it again because it is vital to your success. Pay Yourself First!

Many people think, "I will pay my bills and then what I have left over is going to go into saving." That is a nice idea but it doesn't work.

Please listen to your Uncle Ron. Let me give you an example of why this is important for you and why you have time on your side to make this happen. We have two new graduates; let's call them Mary and Larry.

Mary decides to move back home for a while and gets started saving right away. Larry on the other hand wants to move downtown and wants to spend money on a new car and do some traveling. He says, "I have plenty of time to save for retirement later."

So Mary starts banking her checks and putting money into investments. Here is what happens to both of them.

Mary puts $2,000 away every year for just 7 years and then stops. Larry on the other hand plays for 7 years and then starts putting $2,000 away for the next 20 years and stops. Who will have more 20 years after that? Let's see...

TWO GRADUATES

Mary	Larry	
Starts now	Plays for 7 years and then gets serious	
$2,000	Next 20 years	
$2,000	$2,000	$2,000
$2,000	$2,000	$2,000
$2,000	$2,000	$2,000
$2,000	$2,000	$2,000
$2,000	$2,000	$2,000
$2,000	$2,000	$2,000
Total $14,000	$2,000	$2,000
	$2,000	$2,000
	$2,000	$2,000
	$2,000	$2,000
	$2,000	$2,000
	Total $40,000	

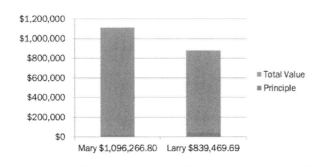

AND THE WINNER IS, MARY!!!!

Mary $1,096,266.80   Larry $839,469.69

Let me illustrate a little further by sharing a bit about my background with you. My father was a man who started several companies over the years and did very well. The lessons I learned over the years of working with and for one of my father's companies are lessons that were infused by doing, not by sitting in a chair and watching a presentation given by a professor. My father didn't give lectures—he took action and I learned by watching. Sometimes I didn't realize what he was doing until many years later.

One of these lessons that I picked up on was based on an event I went to a few years back.

17

It was during the last hour of a three day event (don't leave events early) and the speaker Dan Kennedy was talking to a group of entrepreneurs and the subject came up about how the government's answer to every challenge is that we just need to give more money to the situation. "Our schools are falling behind the rest of the world in math, science, and technology." The government's answer is, "If we had more money..." Then Mr. Kennedy said, "If you can't make money with no money, then you can't make money with money."

The moment he said that, I had a flashback to when my father started the last company he built and he needed a desk. He didn't run out and buy one. Somewhere he found or bought two used, two-drawer file cabinets (one was dented so bad that the drawer barely opened), and then put a piece of plywood over the top. Bam—he had a desk. Call that American ingenuity, or as Larry the Cable Guy would say "Get er done." I always thought he was just being cheap, but I now know that he was getting along with the minimum expenditure to get the job done.

Both of my parents were born just before The Great Depression and that is where much of your parents' and grandparents' investing ideas came from. They were too young to really comprehend what was taking place.

They only remember, believe, and passed on what they saw and picked up as children, which isn't as full a picture of investing (as if they had tried to pick up those same lessons as young adults).

Banks today are considered the pinnacle of safety. But back during The Great Depression many banks failed and people lost all or much of their savings. That is part of the reason we diversify and put money in different institutions as well as different types of investments.

Part of why your parents and grandparents were such great savers is because when they were very young and they were sitting at the top of the stairs listening in on their parents' conversations about money, often times it was about: how are we going to make the house payment or pay for food? Hearing that conversation would scare anyone, especially young people. Back then they didn't give you much slack as to how long after you missed a payment before you were evicted and kicked out of your home.

I do remember one time when I was around six years old my father took us for a ride after he got home from work to show us a family that was evicted into the street. He wanted to show us what it looked like and to scare us into realizing that it can happen to anyone. To this day, I have never forgotten the look of despair on that family's faces.

Now that I have you all bummed out, let's talk about something happy so that never happens to any of you

CHAPTER 4
THE 4 CORNERSTONES OF FINANCIAL PLANNING

I want to do introduce you to what I call, "The 4 Cornerstones of Financial Planning," so you get an idea of where various savings and investments should be positioned in your portfolio.

(This is how I would start my presentations whether I was talking to a large group of people or if I was talking with an individual or couple. Side note, please make sure you and your significant other are both on the same page financially and have the same goals and objectives).

On a piece of paper or on a whiteboard I would write the word "CASH" across the top left quadrant section and start by saying, "this is the first area we are going to cover."

Cash accounts are called things like checking, savings, and money market accounts. Grandma even use to have something called the "passbook account." Today, you might be slightly familiar with PayPal but many know of cash accounts like Venmo, Zelle, and Cash App.

CASH

- Checking
- Savings
- Money Market
- Passbook
- Piggy Bank
- Venmo/Zelle

Good and Not so Good
Liquidity
Value Doesn't Go Down
Lazy Money
The Two Silent Thieves

I would suspect most of you know what a checking and a basic savings account are. You go to a bank or credit union or even use your Venmo account. You put in a dollar in and you get a dollar back (less any fees they charge). You don't have to worry about the value of that account going down due to market fluctuation or volatility.

Sometimes you even earn interest for leaving your money in your account.

There is a good and bad in everything in life and in this case the good thing about money in a cash account is that you don't have to worry about the value of the account going down. Again, you put a dollar in and when you withdraw you get a dollar back.

The disadvantage of money here is that it is, "lazy money." What I mean by that is there are two things attacking our money all the time.

One is taxes and we hear about that all of the time. Every April 15th we have to settle up with Uncle Sam. Actually every paycheck even before we get it, our employer is required to take out a certain percentage and give it to the federal government and state government.

You also have to pay toward something called social security as well as other various entities. The second thing that attacks our money in a cash account is inflation. We hear about inflation all the time. There is even a category where economists predict as to how much inflation there will be each quarter or year.

We hear about inflation so much that we are desensitized to what it actually means. To put it simply, inflation is like a pickpocket, except it doesn't take the whole wallet, just a few dollars more here and there for many different things all the time.

When economists measure inflation they do so in regard to many different things; everything from chandeliers to new cars to new gaming systems.

You want a new cellphone because of all the new features, normally it is going to cost more for the features or for the apps you buy for the phone. Or you go over the data plan and have to pay extra for this month, and it will add up. Here is one example that just happened to me personally. I went to get my car registration renewed and last year it cost around $100 but this year it cost me over $150. That is a 50% increase in just one year!

What you always want to strive do is maintain your purchasing power.

MAINTAINING YOUR PURCHASING POWER

Going to the store; 4 bags of groceries equals $100.

Need to have your money grow so you can keep buying these 4 bags of groceries.

Think of going to the grocery store and for $100 you pick up four bags of groceries. You go back next week and the price won't be much different for the same items (some items may or may not be on sale from week to week). You go back next year and buy the same things that were in the bag from last year and they're going to cost more. That is inflation.

Why is that important? You want to make sure that your money is growing so that you maintain your purchasing power. This is something that happens every year and it doesn't stop. Most likely it won't be the same things that go up every year. It's just that over time just about everything costs more.

25

My mentor, Nick Murry, use to always use postage stamps as his example. If I think back as a kid I could mail a letter for 5 cents but today it costs 55 cents.

While you are working for a living, you will normally try to keep up with or surpass inflation by getting promotions, raises, working overtime, or changing jobs to make more money so it doesn't seem to affect you so much. But when you retire and are on a fixed income it will become more of an issue.

Between taxes and inflation, money kept in cash accounts is safe but shrinking slowly. This is why one should only keep, at most, 3-6 months' worth of living expenses in cash accounts.

If you have something coming up and need to make sure the money is there, like a down payment for a home or college tuition or some other major expense, you may need to keep more money in cash accounts. These are just guidelines.

You want to build up your cash account (3-6 months' worth of living expenses) up as quickly as possible. So, instead of buying a new car or getting an apartment downtown take my advice and live at home or get extra roommates and build up your cash account as quickly as you can.

You'll also want to stop spending money every day on things like coffee or breakfast and lunch. My recommendation as a way to quickly get to your target goal of savings—brown bag it and learn to cook at home. Dinners out should be for special occasions. These suggestions and guidelines will help you get to your target of $10,000 in cash accounts more quickly.

That might sound like a lot of money, and it is, but it will also give you a level of confidence to help you make decisions not out of fear but from the perspective of financial strength.

You will also have created a different mindset for yourself about money and that is to, "think before you spend."

One tip that I will also share at this time is that you need to take on a second job and bank as much of that as possible. The reason for the second job is twofold; first you won't have as much time to spend money on shopping or going out, and second, look at banking away all of that second income right now.

I encourage you to turn the page and keep reading and learning. However, if you find that it's time to call in the cavalry, a financial advisor, especially as we move into higher level personal finance, then I recommend you go for it. An advisor should be someone who is kind, friendly, and helpful, and someone who can provide some fresh perspective to your current and future financial picture.

HOW MUCH TO KEEP IN CASH

Generally, keep 3-6 months' worth of savings expenses.
If you have something important coming up:

    Down payment on a home
    Tuition payment
    Wedding expenses
    Vacation

Tip: *Start building up your cash account, but not at the expense of growing other parts of your savings and investing*

CHAPTER 5
ASSET PROTECTION

The next area we need to talk about is asset protection, or in other words the need to protect the things we cannot afford to be without. This is also another way to describe any kind of insurance.

ASSET PROTECTION

Insurance

Protecting the things you cannot afford to be without.

Health Insurance, Car Insurance, Property Insurance, Life Insurance

The whole idea behind insurance is to transfer risk. When you are young and starting out and if you have a young family you need to have life insurance. You have a lot of future responsibilities and liabilities (school, food, shelter). If you don't make it home to your family, who is going to pay to support them?

If you are single and no one is counting on your future income to help them out, you probably don't need much. That may be temporary. If you are planning to someday have a family, then you may want to purchase some whole life insurance from a mutual insurance company.

The reason for whole life is that it is the most expensive up front but not nearly as expensive in the long run. Think of it like buying a home vs. renting. When you are renting it's less expensive than purchasing a home. When you do purchase a home it's more expensive but you are also building up equity in your home.

Let me explain how life insurance works. There are two major types of life insurance—temporary insurance and permanent insurance.

LIFE INSURANCE

TERM INSURANCE	WHOLE LIFE INSURANCE
• Low Cost/Fixed Benefit	• Costs A Lot More
• Large Amount of Coverage	• Permanent
• Goes for a Specific Period of Time	• Policy Will Pay for Itself After a Number of Years.
• Can Renew but Gets Expensive	• Benefit Will Go Up Over Time
TIP: Suggested Amount of Coverage is 10x Your Current Level of Income	• Builds Cash Value

Permanent insurance is whole life insurance. You buy it and make your premium payments for a number of years and after a time, say for fifteen years, it has accrued enough value to earn what are called dividends (the profits that the insurance company pays back to the policy holders in a mutual insurance company). The policy's dividends will pay for the premium of the policy and potentially buy you more life insurance, which then continues to compound and grow as well.

The other type of insurance you can buy is a temporary insurance, which is very popular today and also referred to as term insurance. Temporary insurance or term insurance is popular because you can buy a lot of it for a little money. Over time though and as you get older it becomes more and more expensive to own, and at some point you may not be able to qualify for term life insurance or even pay a premium (more money) to be insured.

With the cash value in a whole life insurance policy at times you can borrow some of that money and either pay it back or not. If you do not pay it back and you pass away, the insurance company will deduct the amount you have taken out when it pays the claim.

The reason it is called a loan is for tax purposes, so that in essence you are getting a loan that is tax free. If you cash in the policy completely, then you will pay tax on the interest that had accumulated in the policy. So, do yourself a favor and don't cash in the policy completely.

Another type of insurance you may want to consider when you are young is some type of a disability policy because you are more likely to become disabled as opposed to being killed. If you don't believe me go into a nursing home and be prepared to be surprised to see the number of young people there receiving physical therapy. With a disability policy you only get to purchase about 2/3rds of what your income level is but if you purchase it, it comes to you tax free. If your company buys the policy for you, you will pay tax on the whole amount as income. So if you have the option, you will want to buy disability insurance for yourself.

There is another type of insurance called long term care insurance, which generally speaking, will take care of you when you are older. For most people, long term care insurance should be purchased later in life, closer to the age of sixty.

Types of Financial Institutions

Before I go further I want to take a few moments and talk about different types of financial institutions and now seems like a good time to bring them up.

First, many of us know about banks. In the old days they looked like very intimidating fortresses. They were fitted with large vaulted areas and lots of marble and granite in them. The exterior had large columns and the bank's name chiseled into the outside along the top perimeter of the massive structure. When you would see the vault where your safety deposit boxes were, you knew whatever you put in there was going to stay in there.

Banks are corporations. They are in it for the money. Don't get me wrong, I am a capitalist, which means I want companies to compete for my business. When they do that, they often come up with new and popular ways to attract new clients (including you and me) and make money for their shareholders.

This is a point that I don't think gets much discussion. More competition creates more innovation, which creates winners and losers, period. Not all ideas will survive and some businesses will fail, and that is a function of allowing the market to run its course.

Credit unions, on the other hand, are, in essence, owned by the members of the credit union. Credit unions by their nature are designed to help their members and usually offer higher interest rates on their savings and lower rates on loans. Not always, but in theory, that is what they are designed to do.

There are also two other general types of institutions that I need to mention now: insurance companies and investment firms. I will talk a little more about them later but I will just say that the lines have blurred as to what all of these institutions can do now vs. what they use to do many years ago.

Today most financial institutions offer some of the products and services I've already mentioned or have partnered with other organizations to offer pretty much all of the services you need.

The banks answer to the board of directors and the shareholders. Credit unions answer to their board of directors and its members.

It's a slight distinction but one to consider and part of the reason it makes sense to shop around. Sometimes banks or credit unions are trying to grow their assets and will adjust interest rates to attract or repel assets. Often times this is due to what the government is doing when they are changing regulations on these institutions.

So my advice is to always shop around—via an app, bank websites, or with a financial advisor—and see who can give you the best rates or the lowest expenses.

Part II
Loan vs. Own and Advanced Personal Finance

CHAPTER 6
LOANING

Once you have your cash accounts and your asset protection in place you can only do two things with money—you can loan things or you can own things.

TWO THINGS YOU CAN DO WITH YOUR MONEY

Loan   Own

Let's talk about loaning money first.

Loans include: CDs, fixed annuities, and any type of a bond falls into this category as well.

LOAN MONEY OUT

- Certificates of Deposit (CD's) [Bank]
- Fixed Annuities [Insurance Company]
- Bonds [Federal, State, Local, or Corporation]
    Government Bonds AKA Treasury Bills, Notes, Bonds
    Municipal Bonds (Tax Free)
    Corporate Bonds
    Savings Bonds

Let me explain what I mean by a loan by using a CD (certificate of deposit) as an example.

With a CD, you agree to loan the bank a certain amount of money for a certain period of time and you agree on how much interest you are going to charge them. Actually they look at a rate sheet and decide how much interest they are going to pay you.

You say, "I wish it was more," but in the end you agree to lend them the money for a year. That is the term of the transaction.

The bank doesn't just stick the money back into its vault and wait for you to come back in a year.

The bank turns around and lends it out to you for a mortgage or to someone else on a business loan, a car loan, or a credit card.

The difference between what they agree to pay you and what they charge me on say, a business loan, is what they call "the spread," and that's how banks make money.

The same is true with bonds, or whether you loan money to a corporation or the government.

With the actual bond there are a few things I want to bring up. A bond will have what is called the, "face value," meaning this is what the bond will be worth at maturity.

There is also the coupon which is the interest rate that the bond actually pays. Let me share an example. The XYZ Corporation is going to issue a 10-year note at 5% and you decide to buy a $10,000 bond. You will receive a payment of $250 every 6 months and 10 years from now receive your $10,000 original investment back.

With government bonds there are a few types depending on how long you loan them the money.

Treasury Bills are loaned for 3 months, 6 months, or 1 year. You actually buy these at a discount and they mature at face value.

So if you have purchased, say a $10,000 bond, you give them $9,000 and they give you back $10,000 a year from now. That is if rates are 10%, which is nowhere near where rates are today. They are now somewhere closer to less than a half percent for a year (as of May 2020).

So that means you need to give them $9,950 now and they give you $10,000 at the end of the year.

Treasury notes go from 2 years up to 15 years and they are a little different in the way that you pay $10,000 now and at the end of the term when you get your $10,000 back. How you make your money on these is that every 6 months you receive an interest payment based on the interest rate you locked in on that investment.

Treasury bonds work the same way; they just go from 15 years to 30 years.

One other factor that determines what interest is charged depends on the credit rating of the entity. The U.S. government currently earns the highest quality rating which is AAA. The rating goes from AAA, AA, A, and down to Baa, which all are considered investment grade quality. Some institutions can only invest in what is called investment grade bonds. The quality is determined by that entity's ability to make interest payments and pay back the principle at maturity.

Only a small percentage of companies carry investment grade quality—less than 10% of all companies.

The next group of lower quality bonds is classified as "junk." These are going to pay you more interest since there is a higher possibility that they won't make a payment to you or pay your principle back to you (which is your original investment). Generally speaking, they also pay you interest every 6 months.

You may have heard the expression that Mrs. Rockefeller was always clipping coupons. It wasn't coupons from the newspaper for discounts at Walgreens or the grocery store. It was because a long time ago there were actual physical bonds that were created and were made with the same paper that money is made with. There were actual coupons attached to the certificate and you would have to cut them away from the actual bond and take them to the paying agent which was a bank. Whoever physically brought the coupon or bond into the bank at that time would receive the payments.

These were called bearer bonds. This meant that whoever would have physical possession of the coupon or the actual bond at maturity would receive these payments.

Nowadays, bonds are what is called registered, which means that there is no physical certificate issued; there is only an electronic ownership of these bonds.

Most of you might be familiar with a type of bond that is the most widely owned security but the least understood security. These are the U.S. government bonds and you know them as Series EE or H savings bonds.

You buy them at a discount and they mature at face value. So you can pay $25 for a $50 savings bond. These use to take 7 to 12 years to reach maturity. The bonds will continue to earn interest for an extended period of time after reaching maturity.

One of the parts that make it one of the least understood is as to when it pays interest. You can cash it in at any time but it pays out interest every 6 months. This is calculated and paid after the first business day of the month.

That means if you cash it in a day before the interest is paid, you can lose up to 6 months of interest.

There are also what is called municipal bonds (aka "muni bonds") which are bonds issued by a city, county, or state.

The taxes or fees collected by that entity or project are used to pay the interest and principle payments of that note or bond.

One other thing, the interest payments are possibly tax free, so the interest rate that they pay is usually lower, but since you don't pay taxes on it the bond may put more money in your pocket. Here is an example. Say you are in a 50% tax bracket for federal taxes. This muni bond is paying 5% which would be equivalent to a fully taxable bond paying 10%. The fancy term for muni bond's yield is the "taxable equivalent yield" (TEY).

One other thing to point out, if you live in the state that the bond is issued, you may not have to pay taxes on the bonds to the state either.

If you live in a state where there is a high state income tax like California or New York, you need to factor that into your TEY formula to see what your best option is in purchasing a muni bond.

There is also one other factor with a bond that needs to be pointed out and that is if when you lend money to one of these entities—depending on how much other debt they have—and something happens to the entity you may be in line to receive something of the entity's assets if it goes bankrupt or out of business.

Now, let's talk about fixed annuities. With fixed annuities you are loaning money to an insurance company. The benefit you get from this is that you won't pay any taxes on the interest until you pull the money out and start spending it. Also, if you are under 59 ½ you will pay a penalty on it just like an IRA account. So the interest on a fixed annuity is what is referred to as tax deferred.

With an annuity you also have the flexibility of starting an income stream from this, like a pension that can pay you until you pass away or for a specific time period, like five or ten years. Once you elect one of these payment options, then it is no longer flexible; it is pretty much carved in stone, so please weigh these options wisely.

Many people often wonder, "why would I want to give money to an insurance company when the bank is insured?"

That is a great question. If you remember what I had said before—the reason that banks need to be insured is because your money is not in the vault waiting for you to come back. It is out in my mortgage, or in your business loan, or on a credit card. The guideline for banks is that they need to keep $3-$5 in reserve for every $100 that the banks hand out.

The insurance industry does it a little differently. It's called the legal reserve system and what insurance companies do is for every dollar the insurance company takes in, it needs to keep $103-$105 in reserve.

So, if every one of their policy holders comes to the window and wants it all out at one time, technically they can pay everyone back and still have money left over.

The Federal Insurance Deposit Corporation (FDIC) was created after the Great Depression and how the insurance industry held up so well while many banks failed and folded.

That is actually how many people kept going during The Great Depression; they borrowed against the cash value in their whole life insurance policies.

When banks fail, that doesn't mean that the government drives up in a Brinks truck and just starts handing out money.

The government padlocks the doors, so to speak, examines the books and finds a healthy institution to come in and take over those deposits. The name of the bank changes to the name of a healthy bank and things start running smoothly again.

I remember when the Savings and Loan (S&L) Crisis hit back in the early 1990s. Banks along with the government invented a new agency called "The Resolution Trust Corporation" (RTC) and worked out who would take over the S&L institutions until S&Ls no longer existed.

What most people like about money on the loan side of the equation is that they can see a nice slow steady growth like this.

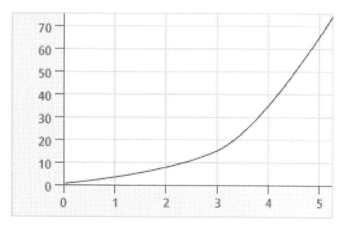

Remember the story of the tortoise and the hare? Slow and steady wins the race. The disadvantage to money here is the two silent thieves. Between the two of them sometimes you may be ahead, but sometimes you may be losing money, in terms of maintaining your purchasing power.

Generally speaking, you don't want to keep too much on this side of the equation especially right now (2020), because it is shrinking, slowly, but it is still shrinking. You also have to factor in where interest rates are within the economic cycle.

When I first started as an advisor back in the early 1980s rates were out of this world. Long term treasuries were paying around 15% and other riskier (lower quality rated) investments were paying even higher.

Remember that XYZ 5% bond that I mentioned earlier? If you experience an annual inflation rate of 3% for a 10 year bond, that $10,000 worth of principle will only be exchanged to buy $7,000 worth of stuff 10 years later. So you do need to make sure that the principle you receive back at the end of the term and interest that you earn will be able to offset that inflation expense and the taxes that you pay on the investment.

LOANS

Good Time to Loan

Best time to loan money out is when rates are high.

Least favorable time is when rates are low.

Bad Time to Loan

CHAPTER 7
OWNING

Now let's start listing things you can own.

OWNERSHIP

Best Time to Own   Rental Property   Rates High

Own Your Own Business

Equities (fancy name for stock)

Variable Annuities

People think investing in stock is like a yoyo, but it's a yoyo on an escalator.

Rates Low   Least Favorable Time to Own

In this category we are going to start off with investments like owning your own business, rental property, equities, (which is a fancy name for stock), and variable annuities.

Investments on this side of the equation generally provide the fastest level of growth with your money over time but it's not this steady arch upward like the loan side. It looks more like this:

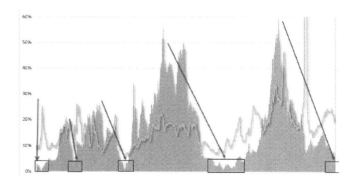

Over time, investments on the ownership side do the best as far as accumulating wealth. What I mean by that is, historically speaking, it will grow faster than inflation and taxes but you need to let it get through an investment cycle.

Generally, it takes 3-5 years to go from the bottom to the top. Many people say it's like a yoyo; it goes up and then goes down. I say it is more like a yoyo on an escalator.

It may go down but it doesn't stay down or go down as low as it did several years ago, and when it goes up, it goes up higher than it ever went before.

One thing most people have never been taught is how or when to buy stock. So, I am going to share with you what I've seen most people do when it comes to buying stock.

49

Just for clarification, when I refer to a stock or buying stock, what you are actually doing is purchasing a tiny piece of a much bigger company. Whether it's in the form of an actual share of a specific stock or within your retirement plans from work or shares of a mutual fund or an exchange traded fund (ETF).

Here is the example I like to share with everyone. Everybody has a brother-in-law or cousin or uncle who is always looking for a "get rich quick" kind of deal.

HOW MOST PEOPLE BUY STOCK

Louie has $10,000 to invest

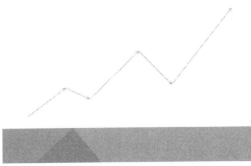

For this example, let's say I have a fictitious brother in law, Louie. Louie comes to me and says he wants to make a lot of money fast, and he wants to do so with stocks. Then he tells me, he has $10,000 and wants to parlay that into a fortune.

The first thing I tell him is that investing in the stock market isn't the best place to try and make a quick buck. He needs to slow down and listen to me.

The first thing I would tell him, like I am telling you, is that any time you put money into the market you have to be prepared to see it go down, like 30%, before it goes up. You aren't going to like that, but you have to be prepared to see that happen and go through the ups and downs of a cycle.

Most people talk about a stock's value rising astronomically—from here to the moon. But they forget to tell you about that side trip it's going to make to China or Timbuktu.

If Louie were real, I would have shared with him one the biggest secrets of investing—it's a marathon not a sprint.

When you buy a stock the first thing that is going to happen is it's going to go down. Just a little bit at first but the closer you watch it or look at it, the more it goes down (it's like it knows that you just bought it).

That is why one of the rules is to only invest money that you can afford to lose. Actually it's not about losing money but it's more a function of having a probability of making money owning stocks.

Back to my example. Against my better judgement, I make a suggestion that Louie should invest in ABC company. It's trading around $10 a share and he could pick up a few hundred shares and still have some money to see if he can find another stock or two to diversify.

I also tell Louie it's not a guarantee, but we could see this stock go from $10 a share to $20 in the next few years due to the management team ABC has in place. ABC has good fundamentals, meaning they make a good product and have a loyal customer base. ABC also has a new version of its product coming out that will take away some market share from some of its competition. They charge a premium for their services, so they are making money and deliver a high-quality product. Plus, they pay a dividend.

Dividends are a portion of the company's profits that it shares with the shareholders. Not all companies pay dividends and it is a big deal when a company starts to pay one. It's only been in the last few years that Microsoft started paying a dividend.

Most small companies instead of paying dividends are in the growth phase and reinvest most of their profits back into the company to help it grow. They hire more people, buy more equipment, open another location—you get the idea. More mature companies allocate a portion of their profits back to their shareholders in the form of dividends.

When considering dividends, you want to look for a company that likes to raise their dividend on a regular basis. For the purposes of my example with Louie, the ABC company has raised its dividend for the last five years and there's no reason to think they won't do it again this coming year. A dividend is also a safety net for a company's stock price and I will explain that to you now.

For simple math purposes, say we are in an interest rate environment where the interest rates on good stocks are paying 10%. So we have a stock that is at $10 a share and it is paying $1 in dividends. That means on average, the price of the stock is yielding 10%.

When stock prices go lower it can be due to a number of temporary factors like some stock made money but didn't make as much as some stock analyst thought it should have, and the price of the stock goes down.

If the stock doesn't pay a dividend, the stock can free fall for a while or take a long time to come back.

But let's use this example and see the stock drop down from $10 per share down to $5. So if the company can still pay their $1 per share dividend, then we have a stock that is paying 20% in a 10% world. The price of the stock is going to bounce back quickly. The company still has enough money in the bank to pay the dividend for a long time and some other analyst sees that this has happened and so it starts buying up shares of a company that is paying 20% in a 10% world. The price of the stock is ready and should start to bounce back.

Conversely, if a company is having trouble with sales, cash flow, or competitors and it announces that it is going to cut a dividend then the price of the stock is going to get hit. Keeping the example of the 10% world of interest rates, the dividend is cut in half. It is likely the stock will also be cut in half if not more, or at least drop in line with what type of yield other dividend-paying stocks are paying.

With dividends and good companies, let's say we have that company raise its dividend from $1 a share to $1.10 and then the next year $1.25 and then to $1.50 the year after that, and we are still in that 10% dividend interest rate world. What would you see happen to the price of stock over time?

We see the price of stock go $10, to $11, to $12.50 and then $15 a share. That's how you grow your wealth over time.

Again, keep in mind these are just examples based on hypothetical interest rates and companies.

With many companies, you can also use dividends to buy more shares of that company stock, often at no or very low cost to you. That's one of the ways you get a compounding effect on stocks.

Back to Louie and my stock recommendation...

Louie hears my recommendation and leaves saying, "okay, thanks, I will think about it."

What happens next is what happens to most people.

They turn around and look at stocks that have just made a ton of money and want to do the same for themselves. Like Louie, they want to make it fast. Not that they can't. It's just the more you need it to happen fast, it's like a gambler—they may wind up ahead for a bit, but they wind up giving it all back, and more!

Louie thinks to himself, "remember Uncle Ron; buy low and sell high."

I talk to Louie the following week and he tells me he went online and opened a trading account. He tells me he has put some money into ZZZ stock that made his buddy some BIG money.

Unfortunately this is what happens all too often. Someone brags about how much money they made in ZZZ and their friend (Louie in this case) wants to make a lot of money so they go ahead and buy some of that same company, which, more often than not, doesn't keep going up.

Louie plunks all $10,000 down on this one stock. I shake my head wondering why he blew everything on one stock.

Louie buys 1000 shares of ZZZ at $10 a share. He found ZZZ when he saw that it was the best performing stock for the previous quarter. It was up roughly 95% in three months. He wanted to make 95% on his money so he jumped on it.

This is not smart investing, which I'll explain in a moment. But this is why you always see the disclaimer, "Past Results are No Guarantee of Future Performance."

Again, what happens when you buy a stock is that it goes down a little. It will go from $10 down to $9—not too much, only a 10% reduction, but then it has to grow to 11% just to get back to even. The more you watch it, the more it goes down.

That is why you should not watch it too closely; it can drive you crazy. For instance, like when you are baking something in the oven, don't keep opening the door to the oven to take a look at how the turkey is doing. Just let it cook.

I couldn't resist the fact that my stock recommendation for ABC went up $2 a share and is now worth $12 a share. Louie would have made 20% on his investment.

You remember the phrase "buy low and sell high." That is true, it's just that the reason a stock is down (or low) is because people don't think or believe a company is going to do well. When a stock is low, not many people want the stock—that is the reason it is so low. You can translate this to: more people are selling the stock than buying the stock. The same happens when stocks go up. It's because lots of people believe there is a great future in the stock. That is how things generally work but there can be other extenuating circumstances.

Fundamentals are one factor but not the only factor. Emotion has a lot to do with it too. There are also factors such as the industry that the stock is in. That is a big influence on what happens to the price of a stock. If one company is big in the news (good or bad) it can affect the price of the shares of other companies in that same industry, especially in the short term.

Let's get back to Louie as far as the two stocks. With Louie's stock, the company didn't meet some analyst's expectation, or projection on the earnings the company should have made (whether the company makes money or loses money that quarter).

Again, it could be for any number of reasons. It could be sales are slow, but it could also be something unrelated. Maybe they ran out of some part for their product that they needed to send out or they were waiting on somebody or something else. It could be they ran out of boxes to ship their products. It could be anything; you don't always know.

That's why it can be a full time job to follow stocks and a reason to have a financial advisor to help guide and advise you. Also, having an advisor helps to keep the "emotion" out of the transaction.

Can you do it on your own? Absolutely! More often than not, it's something that most people should leave to a professional, because it takes up a significant amount of time to watch stocks.

CHAPTER 8
PAYING OFF STUDENT LOANS

One topic that I want to talk about, and one that is going to be a challenge for most people coming out of college today, is your tuition liability.

What I have found as a result of having discussions with many young people, is that most college graduates are leaving school with a tuition bill—aka a tuition bomb—in the range of $25,000 to $50,000 (depending on what school they attended). One woman I spoke with shared with me that between she and her husband, they had a tab of over $250,000 (hers was about $60,000 and his was closer to $190,000 because of his master's degree) which to me is crazy and scary, partly because their degrees didn't set them up for high paying positions after they left school.

Here is what I want to share with you first—shop around to see if you can consolidate and lock-in the historic low interest rates which are available (as of May 2020).

The next thing I would suggest is that you move back home, and/or get that second job and build up your savings muscle. Do your best to save money and build up a $10,000 cushion.

Most people who get a second job will want to pay off their debt as fast as they can. They will also move home and pay extra down on their debt to get it behind them.

After getting a second job and/or moving home, I'd suggest that you don't pay off your tuition bomb as fast as you can. Again, take any extra money and build up your savings and investment account instead. The reasoning behind this is due to what we discussed at the beginning of this book—start saving now and benefit from the compound interest principle. Also what you earn vs. the interest rate you are paying on your loan should be relatively low as of today (e.g. what you earn on your savings and investments should be higher than the interest rate you're paying on your loan).

There's another reason why you shouldn't solely focus on paying down your student loan debt. What happens if you wind up losing your job? You will still have payments and other bills due and you may not have the money to pay those expenses. The third reason you shouldn't focus solely on paying down student loan debt is the principle I shared with you earlier—maintain your purchasing power. What I mean by that is that over time $25,000 to $50,000 in debt won't be as daunting as it is today.

To offset this, your bank account or investment account will hopefully have enough of a cushion to the point that you will still be able to take care of any emergency or expenses.

By following these principles as a template you should have a smoother time paying down your debts while still having a bright financial future.

CHAPTER 9
YOUR RETIREMENT PLAN AND HOW TO GET IT STARTED

Most companies that you are going to work for are going to offer you some type of retirement plan called a 401K plan. If you work for a school or not-for-profit organization you'll be offered a retirement plan called or a 403B plan. These plans come from the Internal Revenue Code and allow you to save money on a pre-tax basis.

This is a shift from businesses in the 1980s that created retirement and pension plans for their employees. Now, more of the responsibility is on the employee (you) and less liability is on the company to make recommendations about investment performance.

Most of the time businesses will offer plans where you put up to a certain amount into the plan each year and what you save is placed into a number of sub-accounts (investment accounts) which you can then select and change your investment choices between a variety of stock and bond options.

Even though you are allowed to deduct the amount you put into a traditional 401K retirement plan, if there is an option to do a Roth version of a retirement plan, you should go with that one. With a Roth you won't get the deduction today, but when you withdraw the money it won't be subject to taxation.

So think of it like this—do you want to pay taxes on the seed or on the harvest? Paying the taxes now will make a huge difference for you in the future.

When you start to put money in this type of plan, most of the time your company will also make some kind of matching contribution so you immediately have a positive return on your portfolio.

Most companies match a certain percentage—they might match 100% of the first 4-6% of what you put away. My suggestion for you is to put in at least 100% of what they are willing to match. That way you automatically enjoy a doubling of your money. Don't leave that money in your company's pocket; make sure it goes into yours.

You may want to add more but at least add 100% of what they are willing to match.

Many times if you have some type of hardship or want to buy a home, you can borrow money from your retirement plan to use without paying taxes. You will, however, want to pay yourself back the money you took out.

If you leave the company for whatever the reason (quit or get laid off) then you will have a taxable event which you will have to deal with.

I don't want to get too deep into this now but make sure you take advantage of this because, it follows the principle I recommended to you earlier which is to pay yourself first!

The Case for Small Stocks vs Larger Stocks

Smaller companies normally will not pay dividends but as I said before smaller companies will continue to reinvest a portion of its profits back into the company to grow.

Sometimes that is a reason you want to buy a larger portion of these types of companies when you are young. You want to use the volatility and another investment principle called "Dollar Cost Averaging" (DCA) to help you grow your portfolio to accumulate wealth and avoid a common investment mistake.

Here is what I mean. Let's say you have $10,000 and you split the investment between two companies.

Company A goes up 50% and company B goes down 50%.I give you $10,000 more to invest, which one are you going to add the money to, company A or company B? Well most of the time, like 95% of the time, you are going to add all $10,000 to the company that went up and 0 to the company that went down.

The truth is it may make sense to add all of the money to the company that went down. That is going to be difficult to do, but, as far as investing, it may make the most sense to add it to the company that went down.

I remember one time I went to talk to an investment club and this is just after we had a meltdown in the stock market and somebody said, "I don't want to add money to the stock market now, it's too risky." I replied, "There is no risk in the stock market now, it's already down!"

The stock market doesn't go down when it is already down 40%. It is more likely to go up from that point, not go down even further.

As I have said earlier, people say the stock market is like a yoyo. It goes up and down. The truth is it's more like a yoyo on an escalator in that it goes down and then it goes up, then it goes down again and goes up higher than it has ever gone before.

That is just a reflection of how the economy rolls. We have good times and bad times.

People think investing in stock is like a yoyo, but it's a yoyo on an escalator.

The stock market doesn't go down big when stocks have already gone down and everyone is hiding in the bushes or making "safe money" types of investments. They go down when everyone is dancing on the roof (like the big tech bubble in the 2000s) because of how much money they made while the stock market was up.

During the tech bubble in the 2000s, some stock mutual funds were up close to over 100%! That's when it's time to get cautious.

With dollar cost averaging (DCA), it takes the emotion out of your investments.

67

Here is an example of how DCAing can help you make money over time.

Let's say you are going to set up a plan and take $100 out of your paycheck and invest that into the market. And let's say that it is going to be a company that is worth $10 a share. So this month you are going to buy ten shares of their company's stock. Next month you invest another $100 but in the past few days the stock market has gone haywire and now the price of that investment is $20 a share. So this month you pick up only five shares. Next month you do the same thing; you add $100 to your investment but that investment has crashed and now the shares are only worth $5 a share, so this month you pick up 20 shares.

Let's do a quick recap and see where you are now.

Month	Amout Invested	Price of stock	NO of shares purchase
January	$100	$10	10 shares
February	$100	$20	5 shares
March	$100	$5	20 shares

TOTALS...........$300.....Average
Price..$11.67/share.....35 shares

Based on this short example here you can see that the average price of what you paid for your stock is $11.67. If the stock stays down and you add another $100 and pick up another twenty shares, your average cost of the shares goes down to $7.27.

Over time this helps you to not overpay when the stock goes up. Unfortunately, though, it doesn't let you buy all your shares at bargain basement prices.

Everyone wants to see their stock go up and I understand that. If you look at this example what you really want to happen is for your stock to go down when you buy it and only go up when you are ready to sell it.

By getting yourself into a regular investment plan, you can accomplish this over time. Keep putting money into your investment and do this first—every paycheck. That is why I suggest getting into a systematic plan of putting money away all the time.

Now comes what I call—how you allocate your portfolio. I'll also explain why it's even more different today than ever before.

When I first became an investment advisor back in the early 1980s, interest rates were historically high with long term treasuries paying around 15% and stocks paying out much (much) lower than that.

The guideline for portfolios was that you took the number 100, then subtracted your age ,and the balance is what you should have on the ownership side of the equation.

That was when grandpa was running around (or when I knew him he was shuffling by then). At this time, grandpa retired around the age of 65 and passed away when he was 72. So he lived in retirement for about seven years.

When he passed away grandma went to live with the kids (usually the oldest daughter). There she lived out the rest of her days.

WHEN GRANDPA & GRANDMA WERE AROUND

Old rule of thumb
Take your age, subtract from 100;
that's the percentage you need to keep on the own.
So, if you are 65 you should have kept 35% on the ownership side.
The reason is when Grandpa was around, he retired at 65.
He received a pension and social security.
Passed away when he was 72.
Lived 7 years in retirement.
Grandma moved in with the kids.

Now, thanks to modern medicine and science, men are living into their mid-eighties and women with the yoga, Pilates, as well as those Peloton bikes, she may never go… And she sure doesn't want to live with the kids; she wants to keep her independence.

Plus with the long term interest rates currently in the 1.5% range (as of May 2020), a year ago they were paying more like 3%. I am going to adjust that calculation to suggest that you take the number 140, subtract your age, and that is the percentage you keep on the ownership side of the equation.

TODAY'S NEW RULES

Factors

- Thanks to modern medicine and science, we've cured everything that kills you fast, but have not helped with what kills you slowly.
  - Men are living into their mid-80s. Between yoga and Pilates, women may never go! (Plus, she doesn't want to move in with the kids).
- Low rates on safe investments.
- Retiring early or companies closing or laying off older workers.
- Higher expenses to live and for medical expenses; also wants to spoil grandkids.

Today's formula (Uncle Ron's suggestion)

Take 140, subtract your age, and that equals the amount you should keep in ownership side of the equation.

140 − Age = % on ownership side.

When thinking about stocks there are also different categories such as large, medium, and small companies. You also have international and global companies you'll want to include in your portfolio.

Again, as you start out and while you're young, look for more volatile and smaller types of company stocks. As you get older and accumulate money start to throttle back and take on less risk and volatility.

Starting your own business like my father did is not for everyone but if you choose to do that let me share a little insight on that.

First, I like the famous quote from Reid Hoffman the founder of LinkedIn. "If you aren't embarrassed by the first version of your product, you've launched too late." Which means get it out there and make adjustments for the next versions.

Another way to say that is version 1.0 is better than no version at all. Too many people, myself included, wait too long to get a version out of their product or business idea out into the marketplace. So my advice to you is—get your first version out there, understand you will make mistakes and then learn from them.

There is no better time to start a business when startup costs are low, especially with an "information business." Plus there is usually more margin in these types of businesses than a brick-and-mortar retail type of business.

Always be frugal when it comes to growing your business. Like the example I mentioned earlier about my dad's desk. One other time he needed to create an office for a new member of his team so he turned a closet in a mailroom into his office and put the coats on a rack in the hallway. He also moved the postage machine and employee mailboxes into the hallway and put them on a card table.

I have books worth of stories about his business acumen and how many times I was embarrassed by how he and his partner kept their expenses low. In hindsight that is how they were able to grow as quickly and as big as they did.

One last piece of advice I will share with you before I let you go. There is an unlimited amount of opportunity in this country and in this world, and the direction you start in more often than not is not going to take you directly to the area that you expect it to. Be flexible and enjoy the struggle, because you will look back fondly on these days as, "the good old days."

Surround yourself with great people. Jim Rohn once said, "you are the average of your five closest friends." So pick your friends wisely; they will contribute to your success.

Thank you.

\-   Uncle Ron

UNCLE RON'S LAST TIPS

- Pay yourself first.
- Get a second job (you'd be surprised how much you save because don't have time to spend).
- Move back home or get an extra roommate.
- Start a Roth IRA.
- If you have the option for a Roth 401K, do it!
- Don't buy a brand-new car (2 years old) also never pay cash for your car.
- Buy quality clothes with classic style.
- Learn to cook.

DEDICATION

There are several people who I would like to acknowledge and thank for their part in this book and in my career.

First, I would like to thank My Lady Barbara for her unwavering support in my life and helping me complete this project. Thank you!

John Egan, who selected me out of 850 original applicants.

To the best sales manager I had in my career, Mike Pasagglia.

My editor, Josh, who cleaned up my original work and made the book flow.

Clint Arthur and Alison Savitch who invited me to speak at NASDAQ, The Harvard Club, and supported me in my professional speaking career.

My great children, Chris, and Erin, who provided the inspiration to complete yet another dream.

Walter Bergeron who has been a shining example of a great business leader.

Big Mike Macchi, my coach and a true inspiration for me.

Mary Q. for her help and feedback.

Maggie and Allison, who gave me the idea for this book.

Liam Crooks who challenged me to finish this book.

Michael Kinnavy for the gentle nudge to getting it done.

Nick Louise who was another shining example of a leader and sharp business man.

ABOUT THE AUTHOR
Ron Penksa

Ron Penksa served as a financial advisor and planner for more than three decades. He was selected from a group of over 850 applicants to join Dean Witter Reynolds in 1984. His progress with Dean Witter took him from Cleveland, Ohio to Rancho Santa Fe, California building his successful career and book of business with "cold calling" for clients. In 1987 Ron broke what was then the world record for cold calling with 1082 dials in twelve hours.

In January 1988, Ron joined Great Western Securities, a subsidiary of Great Western Bank in California, earning him numerous awards including the title of Vice President of Investments, the Sierra Glacier Award, and a member of the VIP Club. Ron was promoted to the position of Regional Sales Manager of the Great Western Sierra Trust Funds covering six states working with brokers and financial planners from many of the country's largest financial institutions.

From 1995 to 1998 Ron launched the most successful "Investment Center" for XCU Capital in Arlington Heights, Illinois. His responsibilities included providing non-traditional investments to members of the credit union.

In 1998 Ron joined Old Kent Bank which became Fifth Third Bank due to an acquisition. While there he set the personal production record for the investment program in 1999 and qualified for the President's Circle in 2000, 2001, 2002, and 2003. This came about by focusing on outside funds (non-bank customers) as well as providing services to bank customers.

In 2006, Ron completed his first year at World Group Securities earning the "Rookie of the Year" award by placing second in personal production and fifth in recruiting within the company.

Ron retired in 2011 after surviving the market meltdown of 2008. Soon, he became bored with doing nothing and started yet another career providing marketing education to small business owners. Today he is utilizing his marketing skills to create a movement to help educate young people to the world of investing, specifically with his new book, The Graduate's Guide to Financial Planning.

Printed in Great Britain
by Amazon